Jeff Bridges

poetry by

Donora Hillard

illustrations by

Goodloe Byron

Cobalt Press
Billings, MT

cobaltreview.com/cobalt-press

For all inquiries, including requests for review materials, please contact cobalt@cobaltreview.com.

Everything is going to be okay.

Jeff Bridges

You have 14 minutes
and then Jeff Bridges.
He lets you win at air
hockey and soaks your
diamonds in No More
Tears. He even holds
your hand after you are
fired for being small.
Happy. You will be happy
and he will give you the
last airplane cookie.
You will look down at the
weird tundra lights,
your America, the thing
with wheels for eyes
growing ever closer.

THE DUDE

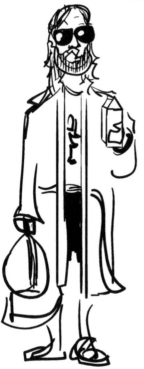

You talk to Jeff Bridges about the blood behind your eyes. He tells you that this is how things got done in the 1990s.

Jeff Bridges

You tell Jeff Bridges you fear
your dying breath will be just like
the whimper you make when trying
to remove glitter polish from your
toenails. He sets his guitar down on
the fur rug. *Baby Sister*, he says,
live like you're already dead.

You try to water fast
because you hate yourself

and Jeff Bridges laughs.
Baby Sister, he says, *why?*

Remember me in FEARLESS.
My hair was so long

and I wasn't afraid
of any strawberry.

I stuck my head out
the window like a beagle.

I yelled at God,
'You want to kill me but you can't.'

So let it go. Let's drive our
Volvo into a brick wall to make

Rosie Perez feel better.
Let's buy presents for the dead.

Jeff Bridges' bald head in IRON MAN shines.
Robert Downey, Jr.'s torso is jealous and afraid.

I am eating animal crackers in bed and you are
in Florida in bed with a new one already or in hell.
Jeff Bridges is in Afghanistan yelling, *Tony Stark
was able to build this in a cave! With a box*

of scraps! The animals look like clouds. Jeff
Bridges would apologize for biting their heads.

Jeff Bridges

Jeff Bridges tickles his aloe plants.
He shivers and farts because
*that shit is poison, man, and better
out than in.* This he tells you
in the voice of God. You walk.
He says you are already dead
and you climb inside his ear.
There is his silver hair,
then an ocean, then a universe.

THE NON-ALIEN GUY IN
K-PAX!

You are sitting at my kitchen table
and Jeff Bridges is in California.
It is either very late or very early.

I am sorry for shaking the table,
for shaking so many legged things.

I kiss your ear and your ear is cold.
I hope that Jeff Bridges is awake
and writing songs about gnats.

STARMAN

You visited for the weekend
        and I am running away with you to Mississippi.
You visited for the weekend
        and I chipped my pedicure on very many walls.

That was overly specific but felt necessary,
        like the gong in Jeff Bridges' driveway.

It was better than you in a hat.
Better than you on a Vespa.

Better than Jeff Bridges
healing that deer with his hands.

BARNEY COUSINS

In THE VANISHING, Jeff Bridges
is the remade villain, even though
Jeff Bridges is typically the miracle

in any given situation. It is 1993,
and Jeff Bridges tries to bury Kiefer
Sutherland alive. Kiefer escapes.

It is 1993, and someone at 20th
Century Fox thinks this is a good
idea. *Het Gouden Ei*[1]. And yet,

you learn. One day, someone will try
to kiss you outside a national disaster
area. You will lose them. Let them.

---

[1] *The Golden Egg*

BAD
BLAKE

In SEVENTH SON, Jeff Bridges throws glitter
at a bear then rides it. Julianne Moore purrs
I love your shoes to her sister-witch, for which you
want to think she will finally win her Oscar.
Jeff Bridges is an old knight. He has always been
a knight, even on his ranch in Montana, even in
dreams. *Fuckin' witches*, Jeff Bridges mumbles
while climbing an epic set of stairs. His back is to
us when he says this because Jeff Bridges has
transcended obscenity; he says, and you believe it,
When you deal with dark, dark gets in you.

Jeff Bridges

At the beginning of ARLINGTON ROAD,
Jeff Bridges rescues a boy who has blasted

his hand into a pulp with fireworks. *Kid*,
Jeff Bridges says to the boy, his mouth agape.

He picks the boy up, makes a tourniquet with
his tie. *Hold on now; you're going to be all right*,

he says to the boy, even though we are all going
to be destroyed quite soon. You want to warn

Jeff Bridges about what is going to happen, his
beautiful 90s panic face lost in the vast machinery:

In the van! In the van! There's a bomb,
in the van, it's got a goddamn bomb!

You have to dream a new America, Jeff Bridges

says, passing out daisies.

You can dance. It's just someone told you not to.

BAD
COMPANY

Jeff Bridges hugs the emaciated young girls in STICK IT
at the Neutrogena National Gymnastics Championship.
When you were that age, you wore a hot pink bikini and
had only eaten oatmeal for what felt like several centuries
on Mars. On vacation, you nearly collapsed at an abandoned
pirate fort. Your family did not notice you swaying against the
bar that separated you from a cliff that dropped into the sea.
Jeff Bridges cares about the girls. *Don't force it, Lacey*, he
says. He gets upset when Mina receives a one-tenth deduction
for an exposed bra strap and argues with the judge, Doris.
*Oh, come on. Doris, she's flipping through the air. She's
spinning, Doris!* And in the end, he tells Haley he is proud
of her, which is all she says she needs. He tells her to floor it.

PRINCE
LiR

Your first memory of Jeff Bridges

                                  was in THE LAST UNICORN. He
played Prince Lir, who stupidly

                              loved Mia Farrow as a unicorn, but
who could ever not love Mia Farrow,

                              whatever she has come to find,
whatever she is in most need of.

                              He slays a dragon, and she does
not care, which makes him the perfect

                              man forever. *My lady, I am a hero*,
he says. *Heroes know that things*

                              must happen when it is time for
them to happen. Anyway, I love you,

                              he says. *That's all I have to tell you.*
That's all I've got to say.

TERRY BROGAN

Sexy Jeff Bridges in AGAINST ALL ODDS
makes you uncomfortable; he plays for a
fake football team called the Los Angeles
Outlaws and is the color of silky caramel.
His name is Terry. You read that Terry
comes from an older Germanic name
meaning "powerful; ruler of the people,"
and that is your Jeff Bridges, although
not in this red car, not talking about mating
under trees. Your Jeff Bridges is the one
who has been married to the same woman
for 40 years, who thinks that what is sexy
is that none of us, none of us, understand
each other. Your Jeff Bridges disappears
into himself at the end of the night, but
not before making sure that everyone makes
it home safely, not before hanging ten.

In 1982, you were born
and Jeff Bridges starred in TRON.
The characters in TRON are meant
to be made of energy and light,
and the problem is that Jeff Bridges
is already made of energy and light,
so the film is quite boring in
the way that life is boring. Still,

you cry thick, salty tears
because someday, he will be gone,
the reality like the small stone
that became embedded in your
foot one summer. But the light
will be left. *Kill your ego and lick
your tears, Baby Sister. Make it happen
as if it's happening for the first time.*

BiG Z

Jeff Bridges realizes that perfection is unknowable. There are some nights he can almost raise his face to meet it, catch it on the air, and on those nights, he looks like a wise old lion. *I'm sorry*, he says, *it's impossible but it's also right in front of us, all the time.*

Jeff Bridges

Never, never, never open the door in the floor.

ROOSTER COGBURN

Jeff Bridges does not have the same black liquid inside him that you do. You see it in an orb at your center, and it is freed by your new husband's voice, your own beating heart. It is the one thing Jeff Bridges cannot help you with. He pats your head. *Baby Sister*, he says. *Everything that I taught you—forget it.*

Jeff Bridges stands big at the end of the world
while you have the sniffles.
This is the story that you will not have a cold forever,
except that one day you will,
and then you will not have to try
anymore.

And won't that be nice?
he says, gazing off into
what you like to call
the middle distance
because it sounds fancy.

Someday.

Jeff Bridges

Acknowledgments

Poems first appeared (often in slightly different forms) in *Birdfeast*, *Cobalt Review*, *Dusie*, *Finery*, *Hobart*, *Rubbertop Review*, and *Vinyl*.

Some lines were adapted from articles that appeared in *Esquire*, *GQ*, *Rolling Stone*, and from John Irving's novel *A Widow for One Year* (as seen in THE DOOR IN THE FLOOR).

For, obviously, Jeff Bridges.

For Keating and Goodloe, for knowing.

About the Author

Donora Hillard is the author of the play *The Plagiarist* (NEA, 2015) as well as *The Aphasia Poems* (S▲L, 2014) and other works of hybrid text, poetry, and theory. Her first full-length poetry collection, *Theology of the Body* (re-released as *Covenant*, Gold Wake Press, 2012) was an Amazon.com best-seller in women's studies in 2010.

Her work appears in *Hint Fiction* (W.W. Norton & Company), *Pedagogy*, *Women in Clothes* (Penguin), and elsewhere, and the projects she has been involved in have been featured by CNN, Lybba, MSNBC, and the Poetry Foundation.

She is a senior lecturer at The University of Akron and lives in Northeast Ohio.

About the Illustrator

Goodloe Byron is a bookist, songist, drawist, and paintist. He learned how to draw by making book covers for such luminaries as Soft Skull Press, NYU Press, Black Mask, and Random House. Much of his youthful energy was lost in a drawn out book adventure in which he left thousands of novels across the world. He learned to draw in order to illustrate said novels, and took up proper painting afterwards, following a freak mural incident in 2011. Since then, he has exhibited artwork near and far, though more near than far.

More from Cobalt Press

Four Fathers: fiction and poetry ($15.00)
Dave Housley, BL Pawelek, Ben Tanzer, Tom Williams
Foreword by Greg Olear

Black Krim: a novel ($15.00)
Kate Wyer

How We Bury Our Dead: poetry ($14.00)
Jonathan Travelstead

Enter Your Initials for Record Keeping: essays ($16.00)
Brian Oliu
Featuring "player two" essays by xTx, Tyler Gobble, Barry Grass, Tessa
Fontaine, Jason McCall, Colin Rafferty, and others.

A Horse Made of Fire: poetry ($12.95)
Heather Bell

Repetition: a novel ($15.00, forthcoming)
James Tadd Adcox

For more information about Cobalt Press publications, including our
quarterly and annual literary journals, visit cobaltreview.com.

CPSIA information can be obtained
at www.ICGtesting.com
Printed in the USA
LVHW081039241122
733869LV00003B/56

9 781941 462140